Original title:
Orange Skies

Author: Victor Mercer

ISBN HARDBACK: 978-1-80586-268-0
ISBN PAPERBACK: 978-1-80586-740-1

The Warmest of Goodbyes

When the sun starts to fling its gold,
It wiggles and jigs without being told.
The clouds wear sunglasses, looking so bright,
As we dance under hues that just feel right.

Your hair's a mixed color, a sandwich spread,
Like jam on toast, or a garden bed.
We laugh as we trip on our shoelace fun,
While seagulls high-five, just out for a run.

The day shimmies on, with giggles and cheer,
Chasing our shadows—the mischief is near!
With a farewell wink, your dog gives a bark,
While the world twirls in its sunset park.

So let's paint the sky with a wink and a grin,
With all of our chaos, and mischief within.
As night brings a curtain, we'll bid it adieu,
With the laughter and warmth, my friend—it's all you!

A Sable Overture

In the evening's big embrace,
A sandwich fell with rapid pace.
The ants took off for the delight,
A feast beneath the fading light.

The sun wore shades of neon glow,
While bunnies jumped, all in a row.
They painted clouds with silly glee,
And played a tune, oh very free.

Hues of Departure

A flying fish forgot its hat,
It landed on a sleepy cat.
The cat just blinked, then chased a bird,
As all the fish began to herd.

The colors danced, a wild parade,
With polka dots and stripes displayed.
A yo-yo sung, a kite did spin,
As laughter bubbled from within.

Twilight's Dance in Cinder

A squirrel tried to twirl and spin,
He tripped and fell, went "Oh, what sin!"
His friends all laughed, so full of cheer,
As shadows fell and dusk drew near.

The moon brought out its disco lights,
As shadows jived in silly sights.
With each footfall, the ground did shake,
In twilight's ball, all hearts awake.

Evaporated Dreams

A dragonfly wore a tiny hat,
While chatting up a friendly cat.
They planned a trip to outer space,
On marshmallow clouds—what a place!

The stars winked down with cheeky grins,
As giggles burst and joy begins.
A galaxy of jello shots,
Where reality forgot the knots.

Horizon’s Warmth

The sun slips down, a drowsy face,
Chasing clouds, a silly race.
Birds in frenzy, chirp and jest,
A sunset dance, nature's fest.

Hot dogs sizzle, mustard flies,
Laughter echoes, joyful sighs.
Neighbors wave, a friendly call,
As day takes a playful fall.

The Tapestry of Twilight

Brush strokes bright, the canvas bright,
A child’s giggle, an early night.
Cats parade, with tails held high,
Each one plotting a sneaky spy.

In every yard, a grill’s allure,
Burgers bounce, they want a tour.
Fireflies blink in a crafty way,
The evening scoffs at daytime's play.

Twilight's Golden Breath

A banana peel, a slip, a grin,
As laughter erupts, the fun begins.
Kids on trikes zooming past,
Chasing shadows, oh so fast!

On the porch, old folks share a jest,
Retelling tales, they feel the best.
Stars peek out, the night's a stage,
A comedy act, with every age.

Cascades of Burnish

A squirrel with acorns makes a mess,
In the park, it's anyone's guess!
Giggling children, frozen in awe,
At a dog that just won't obey the law.

Here comes the ice cream, a chilly cheer,
As sticky fingers hold it dear.
With each drip, we laugh aloud,
At the sweet chaos, we are proud!

Gloves of Sunset

The sun slips on its gloves,
It's time to play outside,
With fingers dipped in gold,
And laughter as our guide.

We slide down rainbow roads,
With candy dreams in tow,
Chasing shadows that giggle,
While the breezes blow.

The clouds wear silly hats,
With puffs of fluffy glee,
They dance around the sunset,
A sight that's pure esprit.

In the twilight's warm embrace,
We'll spin till we both fall,
The sky's a jester now,
And we're its silly thrall.

Woven in Warmth

As day plays hide and seek,
With hues that twist and twirl,
We're wrapped in laughter's quilt,
A patchwork boy and girl.

The sky smiles all around,
In shades that tease the eye,
Telling jokes with colors,
That make the seagulls cry.

We toast marshmallows bright,
In flames of giggling cheer,
As the fabric of the sky,
Stitches jokes for all to hear.

Woven tight in sunset,
The world begins to glow,
Life's a funny blanket,
With threads of bright hello.

The Sizzle of Sundown

The sun cooks up a feast,
In a pan of painted blue,
With splashes of tomato,
And a side of silly stew.

Grasshoppers crack a joke,
As they hop from leaf to leaf,
While squirrels plan a party,
To celebrate our belief.

A sprinkle of admiration,
On top of giggling rays,
Is served with a slice of joy,
To end these golden days.

The sizzling of the twilight,
Whispers tales of delight,
So grab your fork and dance,
In this quirky fading light.

Celestial Oranges

The heavens are a kitchen,
With fruits drifting near and far,
A giant throws a party,
Using planets as his jar.

Tangerines in spacesuits,
Juggling stars with flair,
While galaxies all giggle,
At the comets rushing there.

We toast to cosmic nectar,
With glances through the haze,
As meteors drop jokes,
In the middle of their phase.

With laughter in the cosmos,
And colors on the breeze,
The universe keeps dancing,
In sweet celestial tease.

Illuminated by a Flare

A crow with shades struts on the lane,
Sipping soda, dodging the rain.
Pizza delivery rides on a bike,
Bouncing along like a wannabe dyke.

A dog in a tux, ready to dance,
He twirls with a cat; it’s a wild romance.
Laughter erupts from pickleball games,
While everyone pretends they’re not to blame.

Twilight's Fluid Palette

The trees are gossiping, throwing shade,
While squirrels debate if it’s too late.
Fireflies are buzzing, dressed up for fun,
Trying to outshine the setting sun.

A raccoon wearing socks breaks into a spin,
The moon looks confused; does it let him in?
Ice cream cones melt on a swing set high,
As kids giggle wildly beneath the sky.

Sunrise in Reverse

The sun yawns wide, ready to snooze,
As coffee sips dance in morning hues.
Pajamas parade on sleepy feet,
While toasters spit toast at a wild beat.

A rooster plays hopscotch, looking absurd,
With a jazz band of ducks, you've heard every word.
Morning glories bloom with a wink,
As laughter still lingers around the kitchen sink.

Day's End Glimmers

A cat on a roof starts to croon,
Under the watch of a big round moon.
Neighbors’ barbecues smoke like a scene,
While kids launch rockets made of cuisine.

Frogs in bow ties throw a night bash,
With swirls of confusion and a big splash.
Lemonade pours while the stars dance and prance,
In a neighborhood where nobody can take a chance.

Brilliant Aura of Dusk

The sun slips down, a playful tease,
Dancing rays that bring you to your knees.
Clouds wear shades like a wild parade,
While birds in wigs perform their charade.

A golden giggle breaks into a grin,
As shadows stretch, let the magic begin.
Fireflies join with their tiny lamps,
Igniting laughter in grassy camps.

Horizon's Fiery Embrace

A pizza's hue fills the sky so bright,
It’s lunchtime fuel for a daring flight.
With cheese and crust from the heavens above,
The world looks tasty, all warmed with love.

As the sun winks with a flaming red eye,
Clouds become marshmallows floating by.
The horizon sizzles like bacon in a pan,
And every wink brightens up the land.

A Symphony of Sunset Colors

The sky's a canvas, splashed with glee,
Silly shades like a clown's jubilee.
Pink and purple play hopscotch on high,
While the sun throws confetti to the sky.

A jazzy hum in the air's delight,
Dancing colors that twirl, taking flight.
Even rainbows giggle, so bold and spry,
As the day turns backflips, oh my, oh my!

Glowing Reflections

A mirror splatter, all winking bright,
The world's a stage in the twilight light.
Splashing hues like clowns at a fair,
With shoes too big, they leap through the air.

Ripples of laughter bloom on the lake,
As ducks join in for a quacking break.
The glow invites all to paint with cheer,
Reflect on fun, let the silliness steer.

Saffron Reflections

The sun's a giant tangerine,
It rolls away with gleeful glee,
The clouds are laughing on the scene,
They tickle each other, can’t you see?

A squirrel took a jump, so bold,
He thought he’d touch that fiery hue,
But landed in the marigold,
His tail’s now painted bright and new!

The sky sighs softly, doing tricks,
With whipped cream clouds and jellybeans,
We all join in, what a good fix,
With sugary dreams and silly scenes.

In twilight, we shall dance and play,
With kooky hats and neon ties,
As constellations groan and sway,
While giggling softly in the skies.

Celestial Hearth

In evening’s glow, the stars peeked out,
Like tiny oranges in a stew,
They popped and danced, oh, what a shout,
As the moon donned a silly shoe!

A comet sneezed, and sparkles flew,
The night got startled, jumped with fun,
The cosmic laughter, oh so true,
Made shadows waltz 'til morning sun.

The Milky Way, a creamy swirl,
With marshmallow fluff and space confetti,
A swirling dance, a cosmic whirl,
The universe got really petty!

So grab a friend and laugh away,
Watch dreams take flight on satin beams,
In a hearth of giggles, come what may,
We’ll share our silly cosmic dreams.

Rust and Gold

The sun is rusting on the line,
With copper blush and tales to tell,
Gold giggles sprout in joy divine,
As day wears its sparkly shell.

The breeze is playing peek-a-boo,
Tickling leaves and chasing light,
A rusted bike rides with a view,
As butterflies take flight with might!

Old fences creak with tales of yore,
Like wise old friends who laugh and sigh,
As squirrels conduct a merry score,
Rust and gold dance, oh my, oh my!

So let’s make fun of aging stars,
In this jovial twilight lark,
Let’s paint the cosmos with our jars,
Sprinkle laughter, light the spark!

A Glimpse of Ember

The horizon spills its peachy blush,
As fireflies play tag with dusk,
A cat in shades, all in a rush,
A funny sight, just like a musk.

A flamingo struts in polka dots,
With flip flops on, oh what a scene,
Believing he's a lucky spot,
With dreams of fruit and tangerine!

The fade of day brings giggles bright,
As shadows chase the sun away,
A canvas painted up in light,
Where every wiggle makes us sway!

So join this wild and dandy ride,
With fizzling stars and silly charms,
In the warmth of evening, side by side,
We'll dance in joy, with open arms!

The Farewell Glow

The sun sends off a cheeky grin,
As clouds wear hats, a silly win.
A parrot dances, wings a-flap,
While squirrels plot their evening nap.

Frogs in bow ties start to croak,
Joking with the evening smoke.
Crickets play a jazzy tune,
As fireflies wink beneath the moon.

Horizon’s Lament

The sun dips low, a clumsy feat,
Tripping over tomatoes, oh so sweet.
A wise old owl hoots with glee,
“Why so bright? Just let it be!”

Clouds gossip like a lively bunch,
“Is he leaving? Let's all munch!”
Laughter echoes in the breeze,
As ladybugs play cards with ease.

The Burst of Day’s End

A pop! A fizz! The colors flare,
Like jellybeans tossed through the air.
The sky's a canvas, splashed and bold,
Silly giggles from the gold.

A cat in shades lounges with flair,
As butterflies dance without a care.
“Catch me if you can!” they tease,
While bats complain, “Oh, such a breeze!”

Fiery Euphony

A band of clouds, a rocking show,
Strumming strings of blazing glow.
A sunbeam winks, a playful tease,
While shadows shimmy in the breeze.

Giraffes tap dance in the dusk,
With giraffe hats, oh, what a fuss!
The moon rolls in, all smug and sly,
"Try to top this, oh my, oh my!"

Flare of the Evening Star

The sun winks down, a cheeky grin,
Painting the clouds, let the fun begin.
A parrot's squawk, a singing lute,
As squirrels dance in their nutty pursuit.

With a wink from the moon, night takes a bow,
While crickets chirp, and shadows avow.
Fireflies flash like disco balls,
And laughter rises, as fun befalls.

A dog on a skateboard zooms by fast,
While a cat in sunglasses is having a blast.
This splendid show, a grand soirée,
Where mischief reigns until the first ray.

So raise a toast to this twilight spree,
With giggles galore and wild esprit.
Under this canvas where silly rules,
Life’s just a sitcom played by the fools.

A Fire Within

In the oven, a pie makes a steamy show,
With cheeky squirrels peeking, all aglow.
A dance-off sparks in the kitchen bright,
As spatulas twirl, preparing for night.

The oven beeps with a playful tune,
While cats plot snacks beneath the moon.
Baked treats rise with a bouncy cheer,
Can't wait to share with each comical peer.

The marshmallows boast of their fluffy fame,
While cookies argue about who's to blame.
A riot of flavors, a sweet, baked sin,
Laughter erupts with each clever grin.

So gather 'round, the feast is near,
With friends and giggles, our hearts will steer.
For in this kitchen, joy takes flight,
With a fire that warms through the silliness of night.

The Night Awaits

Under a blanket of twinkling lights,
A troupe of ducks prepares for flights.
With giggles and quacks, they start to rise,
Finding mischief in the velvet skies.

The stars play hide and seek with the moon,
While a raccoon tries to hum a tune.
Banshees and owls join in the fun,
As the night's laughter has only begun.

The shadows dance with a comical flair,
While the crickets debate who best feels the air.
Lamp posts giggle, their lights in a jig,
As fireflies twinkle, their glow is so big.

So let's frolic and trip as the hour grows late,
In this wacky world, we celebrate fate.
For under this blissful, whimsical spell,
The night awaits, with stories to tell.

Hearth and Sky

Gather 'round the warm, cozy flame,
With friends who are perfectly silly, not tame.
The logs crackle with a popcorn pop,
As stories twist and twirl, never stop.

With blankets all piled like a fluffy heap,
The stars above giggle, their secrets to keep.
A marshmallow debate: charred or just hot?
In the night's fun wrestle, every bite's a lot.

The moon throws laughter like confetti in air,
While squirrels!

giggle, all light as a spare.
As jokes fly faster than a comet streak,
In this playful orbit, we all feel unique.

So here's to the cuddle, the jest and the cheer,
With hearts full of warmth as we draw ourselves near.
In the hearth's bright glow and the sky's quirky sigh,
We find a world where silliness will never die.

Sky’s Last Dance

The clouds were doing the cha-cha,
As the sun kicked off its shoes,
With a wink and a silly grin,
It twirled like it had nothing to lose.

Birds joined in with a quack and a flap,
They formed a conga line, oh so spry,
A disco ball spun from cotton candy,
While breezes whispered a goofy sigh.

The trees began to sway along,
Swinging limbs like they were on stage,
Laughing leaves played peekaboo,
As twilight started to engage.

And as the lights began to dim,
The sky took a bow, then waved goodbye,
Leaving behind a pinkish glow,
That made the stars giggle and sigh.

The Burnished Embrace

The canvas stretched in vivid blends,
As laughter popped like fizzing drinks,
With the sun in a top hat, so grand,
It played tricks, or so it thinks.

Squirrels donned their fancy coats,
Chasing dreams on a park bench,
While ants were having a parade,
Waving flags with a sunburnt quench.

Every blink was a burst of cheer,
As if candy was falling from the air,
The grass wore a playful shade of gold,
With giggles threaded everywhere.

The horizon chuckled, so amused,
By the antics of day's silly phase,
Until night swooped down with a grin,
And tucked the sun in, just for a daze.

Twilight's Searing Kiss

The day kissed night with a smooch,
So bold that it made flowers blush,
Crickets laughed, chased by a breeze,
As shadows danced in a secret hush.

Fireflies wore glow-in-the-dark ties,
Flying high, making the streetlights frown,
While the moon took selfies in the sky,
Sporting a crescent shaped crown.

The sidewalk chalk drew its own map,
As twilight sprawled on the concrete, wide,
With giggles echoing down the lane,
Where time slipped by with a lollipop glide.

And just when you thought it was done,
The stars broke in like an eager guest,
Sipping starlight from a teacup,
As the world wore a dreamy vest.

Dappled Evening

The shades of twilight fluffed their coats,
In patches like a playful quilt,
While jokes about squirrels filled the air,
As every critter here was built.

The wind whispered tales of the day,
Tickling flowers, making them sway,
And lanterns flickered into life,
With a wink, they breathed, 'We're here to play.'

Caterpillars told aspiring dreams,
While the sun played its final song,
Charming the sky with giggly hues,
A rhapsody twinkling all night long.

With skies dappled in hints of cheer,
The world erupted with sparkle and grace,
As night draped in its comfy shawl,
Leaving laughter in every space.

The Warm Embrace of Evening

The sun dips low with a wink,
Clouds gather for a quick drink.
Lemonade clouds, what a sight,
Time for silliness tonight.

The birds don hats, quite a show,
They prance and dance to a glow.
Squirrels wear shades, so divine,
Claiming the dusk as their time.

Fireflies twinkle in delight,
Practicing moves in the night.
All the world looks like a clown,
As colors laugh and swirl around.

When giggles bubble in the air,
And shadows play without a care.
Evening giggles fill the sky,
With silly dreams as stars pass by.

A Burst of Colorful Whimsy

Paint the sky with a splash and dash,
Cats on stilts make quite the splash.
A jester's cap on the moon's bright face,
As clouds play tag in a wild race.

Colors swirl like a carnival,
Balloons giggle, they're havin' a ball.
Sunsets strut in polka dot hues,
While the universe sings silly blues.

The trees wear slippers, oh what fun,
As butterflies dart, dances begun.
Jellybean rain from a canvas above,
Brings giggles and chuckles, a push and a shove.

A kaleidoscope marriage of cheer,
The whimsy flows, it's perfectly clear.
Life's a joke that we all can share,
In this magical moment, nothing to spare.

Radiant Horizons

Balloons bounce in the bright horizon,
Where goofy giggles are surely risin'.
Marshmallow clouds with smiles so wide,
In this land of laughter, we all glide.

Llamas wearing shades strut with style,
Their quirky antics make us all smile.
Hopping in rhythm, a cheeky parade,
As colors mingle in a playful cascade.

The sun does cartwheels, oh what a sight,
Twinkling yellow in sheer delight.
Tacos float by on a fluffy breeze,
Join in their dance if you please.

With all the hues of a silly scheme,
Reality turns to a whimsical dream.
Let’s capture this moment, joy’s alight,
In this radiant realm where laughs unite.

Dusk's Fiery Embrace

As the day wears a bright boa,
The stars come out for a joyful show.
Crickets chirp with a flippant cheer,
In the twilight glow that draws us near.

A raccoon winks, with flair galore,
His antics leave us wanting more.
Sundaes float on puffy clouds,
While laughter bursts where fun enshrouds.

The colors wrestle in a jolly fight,
Gold and pink in a comical flight.
Fireworks giggle with each boom,
Lighting up the sky, dispelling gloom.

In this riot where silliness dwells,
As nature shares her quirky spells.
Let’s dance with dusk, the world’s embrace,
In this zany circus, find our place.

Golden Hour Echoes

The sun is playing peek-a-boo,
With clouds that dance a silly hue.
The world is wrapped in a golden glow,
Even the cats seem to steal the show.

Birds are chirping witty tunes,
While squirrels prance beneath the moons.
A dog attempts a daring leap,
But slips and lands in a pile of sleep.

Children giggle as they race,
Chasing shadows in a playful chase.
The lemonade stands are all around,
With sticky fingers and joy unbound.

As the day slips into night,
We laugh until it feels just right.
With every echo, every cheer,
We toast to fun, all gathered here.

Saffron Dreams in the Air

A frisbee sails through the dizzy sky,
As grandma shouts, 'Hey, don't be shy!'
The ice cream truck rolls down the lane,
With flavors that can drive you insane.

Balloons are stuck on the dog’s big nose,
He chases after, but, oh, how it goes!
The little ones giggle, the parents frown,
As the pooch becomes the jester of town.

The sun begins its playful dive,
Where all the buzzing insects thrive.
Picnic ants march in a line,
Stealing snacks and feeling fine.

Saffron dreams float in a swirl,
Tickling senses, making us whirl.
With laughter loud and spirits high,
Every moment is a sweet goodbye.

Candescent Constellations

Stars are twinkling like a disco ball,
While puppies give their best glaring call.
Up in the sky, a comet zooms by,
And kids all gasp with a joyful sigh.

Fireflies wink with a cheeky glint,
As if they know just the right hint.
A scientific debate breaks the night,
'Is that the moon or a brightly lit kite?'

Chasing their dreams in the softest light,
The night is filled with pure delight.
With sleepy heads and candies to share,
We make wishes on laughter and flare.

In every corner, stories unwind,
With silly dances and hearts that bind.
Candescent hopes rise like the stars,
Reminding us life is full of bizarre.

The Warmth that Lingers

As sunflowers stretch for the last warm rays,
We dance our goofy little ways.
In the garden, tomatoes burst with glee,
Still wrestling over who gets the last pea.

A kite tangled high in a tree so green,
Becomes the talk of the neighborhood scene.
While Grandpa's stories bring giggles galore,
Of when he lost his pants at the shore.

Marshmallows roast with a crackling sound,
Everyone's joy simply knows no bounds.
As shadows grow long, we gather round,
With jokes and laughter, our hearts unbound.

In every moment, friendship flows,
In the warmth that lingers, laughter grows.
As stars begin to take their stand,
We hold on tight, hand in hand.

The Day's Farewell Hue

The sun wears shades so bright and bold,
A cloak of tangerine, a sight to behold.
Clouds gossip softly, a silly crew,
Discussing who looks best in this funky view.

A rubber duck floats in a puddly spree,
While shadows laugh and dance with glee.
The trees lean in, they've got jokes galore,
As daylight winks and gets ready to snore.

Crickets start their band, it's quite the scene,
With twilight strumming the ukulele's sheen.
Everything sparkles, the moon claims a throne,
In a realm where sunset and giggles are known.

So grab your popcorn, settle in tight,
For the evening promises a whimsy-filled night.
You'll chuckle with stars, so don't run away,
In this carnival glow, let's dance 'til the day!

A Ballet of Colorful Rest

The horizon flaunts a tutu of flair,
As day pirouettes without a care.
Ballet shoes on clouds, they twirl and spin,
In a comedy show, let the laughter begin!

A flamingo struts with a mix of pride,
Lemonade sips from the sun's bright side.
While daisies shimmy in golden delight,
Chasing away all remnants of fright.

The light takes a bow, it's done with the race,
As giggly shadows take its place.
Fireflies jump into the limelight,
In this quirky dreamstate of whimsical night.

So embrace the colors, let laughter unfurl,
Join this quirky, fun-loving swirl.
As the day whispers secrets, into the fold,
We'll giggle and twirl in shades loud and bold!

Light's Last Dance

The sun dips low, a wink in its sway,
Twirling clouds in a playful display.
The colors clash in a silly parade,
While birds burst into laughter, unafraid.

A kangaroo hops, not wanting to settle,
With a sunset maraca, it taps on the metal.
Each shiny star feels a tickle of glee,
While cheese-colored moon joins the jamboree!

The landscape is painted with whimsy and cheer,
As everything giggles, it’s all so sincere.
The day's last laugh echoes, a joyous refrain,
In this vibrant fiesta of one final gain.

So gather your smiles, watch the light glide,
In a jubilant mix where fun cannot hide.
Let's toast the adventures before night takes flight,
Reveling in colors that dance with delight!

Serenade of the Setting Sun

The sun hums a tune, all jazzy and bright,
While clouds play maracas, taking flight.
They shimmy and swirl in this musical bliss,
Sending giggles and joy, wrapped up in a kiss.

The mountains tap their toes, joining the fame,
As squirrels channel the beat, dancing their game.
They wiggle and jiggle in gleeful embrace,
In this serenade twilight, a whimsical space.

The water reflects a riot of hues,
As fish chuckle softly, sharing their views.
Fireflies like dancers flitter about,
In this whimsical show, there's never a doubt!

So raise a toast to the end of the day,
In this funny ballet that’s here to stay.
For as shadows grow long, our laughter will swell,
In the serenade of dusk, all’s joyful and swell!

Twilight's Ember Glow

When the sun decides to pout,
Colors spill, they dance about.
Clouds wear hats, a silly sight,
As day turns slowly into night.

Lemonade skies and tangerine,
Giggles float where birds convene.
The horizon grins, it's quite absurd,
A mime performs without a word.

Jokesters paint with brushes wide,
Silly shapes that drift and glide.
Every ray a punchline bright,
As laughter wraps the fading light.

At dusk, the world becomes a jest,
With hues that surely know the best.
So gather 'round, let worries go,
And revel in the twilight's glow.

The Canvas of Dusk

On the palette of the skies,
Giggling clouds in a twisty rise.
Smiley suns play peek-a-boo,
While birds crack jokes, both old and new.

Brushstrokes thick, a funny blend,
As day and night start to pretend.
With every shade, a playful fight,
The canvas chuckles, pure delight.

Popsicle hues and sherbet rays,
Frolicking through the sun’s last gaze.
Tickling cheeks with a breezy hand,
Nature’s whimsy, a grand stand.

When stars pop out like jolly beans,
The moon laughs softly, or so it seems.
Let’s dance until the darkness grows,
Underneath the painted glow.

Sunset Whispers

As the light begins to frown,
The sky wears a clown's big gown.
Citrusy hues in cheeky flight,
Giggles echo through the night.

Pineapple pink and raspberry blue,
Splashing laughter, a charming view.
Each whisper from the sun’s retreat,
A playful prank, a funny treat.

The clouds exchange their silly jokes,
While crickets start their evening pokes.
A blanket spread for all to share,
Where chuckles dance upon the air.

With every turn, the skies conspire,
To keep our hearts forever higher.
So grab your friends, join in the mirth,
The sunset’s giggle warms the earth.

Celestial Apricot Dreams

In the twilight, fruit floats on by,
Apricots giggle from the sky.
Whiskers twitch on clouds so fluffy,
As stars show off their magic duffy.

A moonbeam’s wink, a comet's grin,
Silly sprites begin to spin.
Chasing colors in a whirlwind,
With every blink, the fun won’t end.

Candy-coated thoughts appear,
Marshmallow laughs, they disappear.
As day takes leave with a happy cheer,
The night rolls in without a fear.

So revel in this sweet ballet,
Where all your worries fade away.
In dreams of apricot delight,
We live and laugh in starry night.

Citrus Clouds in Flight

In a world of citrus dreams,
Fluffy clouds like ice cream beams.
Lemon drops and tangerine,
Spread over fields of vibrant green.

Silly birds in shades of zest,
Dress up fancy for a quest.
They break dance on fluffy fluff,
Waddling around, they can’t get enough.

Picnics planned on sunny nights,
Juicy laughs and fruity fights.
The sun laughs, its rays so spry,
Tickling the cheeks of passersby.

With capes they twirl in grand ballet,
Mango flies through a zesty spray.
In this realm, we'll take a ride,
On citrus dreams, enjoy the slide!

Radiant Reverie

Underneath a lemon glow,
Silly shadows dance and flow.
A grapefruit wiggles 'round the bend,
Spreading joy, our fruity friend.

Peachy laughter fills the air,
A wispy cloud with citrus flair.
Singing songs, they swap a tune,
Bouncing as if on a big balloon.

Here, the sun wears a silly smile,
Winking for just a little while.
Dance with nuggets of candied light,
Let’s twirl and leap through the night!

In this land where flavors clash,
Giggling figures in a dash.
We’ll ride the storm and twist our fate,
In radiant joy, let’s celebrate!

Caramel Horizons

As the day dips low and sweet,
Caramel drips beneath our feet.
Giggling squirrels with candy eyes,
Chase after dreams beneath candy skies.

Cotton candy held so tight,
Turns the world into pure delight.
Chocolate rivers flow with glee,
And gummy bears join us at the tea.

The sun, it winks with cheeky glow,
While sprinkles dance just like a show.
We sail on clouds of butter scotch,
In a whimsical caramel swatch.

Oh, the laughter in every bite,
Wraps us up in joy tonight.
Chasing colors, laughing wide,
On this joyous, candy ride!

Evening's Fiery Brushstroke

With a brush dipped in cherry bliss,
The sky paints chaos, can you miss?
Jumbling colors, playful art,
Evening's giggle plays its part.

A tangerine jester swings about,
Making rainbows dance, no doubt.
Fireflies join this merry spree,
Twinkling lights on a fruity sea.

The clouds sport hats like pineapple,
Stirring up a tasty grapple.
With a wink and a swirl so bright,
They tickle shadows, oh what a sight!

As laughter swirls on gentle gusts,
Juicy dreams become our musts.
In this painting of endless fun,
The day bids cheer before it’s done!

Firelight Above the Horizon

In the evening glow, all critters prance,
A squirrel wears a hat, thinks it’s a dance.
Chasing shadows, they leap and collide,
Under a sky that’s a wild joyride.

The sneaky cat thinks it's a sunset stage,
Pawing the clouds like they’re on the page.
With dreams of being a star in flight,
As fireflies laugh, igniting the night.

A dog on a leash, spins like a top,
With a wagging tail that just won’t stop.
The birds join in with their silly songs,
Under this lantern where laughter belongs.

The sun takes a bow, it’s time to halt,
As giggles echo, no one thinks of fault.
So with a wink, they all bid adieu,
To the spectacle made of laughter and hue.

A Tapestry of Tangerine

The jellybeans scatter, all colors collide,
In a canvas of sweetness, it’s quite the ride.
Cotton candy clouds swirl in a twist,
As licorice whips at the tongue like a fist.

A parrot on a swing, squawking in glee,
Claims the sunset as its personal spree.
Mice in tuxedos are waltzing along,
With a tango of cheese, it’s where they belong.

Silly flip-flops chase each other around,
As shadows play tag on the dancing ground.
A rabbit sports shades, cool as can be,
In this vibrant scene, oh what a spree!

With laughter as bright as a paint-splattered sky,
In this playful realm where giggles fly high.
As colors blend into a riotous cheer,
A tapestry woven from joy and sheer.

The Last Light's Serenade

Sunset whispers secrets, a laugh shared with trees,
As kids chase their shadows just buzzing with glee.
Lemons and limes in a playful debate,
Who's the juiciest fruit at this sunset rate?

A goat in a tutu, twirling with flair,
As crickets compose, a band in midair.
The moon peeks out, wearing a sly grin,
For a starry duet, the show shall begin.

With hummingbirds zooming to catch all the tunes,
While lazy dogs nap in the light of the moons.
A deer cracks jokes with a wise old owl,
As candy floss shapes make the softest vowel.

The evening wraps up, but laughter stays bright,
With cheeky remarks until far into night.
In this serenade of silliness' reign,
Every farewell is just laughter again.

Hues of Melting Sorbet

The sun drips down like a scoop of delight,
While penguins in shades have a frosty fight.
Pineapples dance on the sand with a twist,
In a fruity parade that no one can miss.

A tricky raccoon crafts a sun hat of fluff,
As seagulls engage in their rowdy enough.
With spoons made of waffles, they dig in with mirth,
On this carnival of flavors, there's nothing like worth.

Chinchillas in blenders mix up the fun,
As flavors collide under a cheeky sun.
With gingerbread sailors in boats made of pie,
Each wave of dessert makes you laugh till you cry.

At dusk, they rejoice, their palates so light,
With the last of the sorbet, all dance in delight.
For in this wild whimsy of tastes to explore,
Every giggle is sweet, and they always want more.

Tints of Day's End

The sun dips low, what a sight,
With coffee cups clinking, oh so bright.
The clouds are like cotton candy folds,
As laughter fills the air, pure gold.

A dog in sunglasses chases a cat,
Both plotting the end of the day just like that.
The trees wear a blush, all dressed up right,
In the grand parade of this silly night.

Neighbors compete in a dance-off spree,
Who knew the old man had moves like a bee?
The skies turn pink, then a lovely peach,
As everyone here reaches their fun-filled peak.

With giggles and wobbles, we all take flight,
Floating like balloons, nothing feels tight.
As day’s end whispers like a playful tease,
We’ll sip on joy under such warm, fuzzy pleas.

The Alchemy of Dusk

Dusk arrives with a wink and a grin,
Turning the world like a magic spin.
The streetlights flicker, one after one,
It's a weird, wacky race, oh what fun!

The squirrels are planning some sunset heist,
While birds joke around, with laughter spiced.
The shadows stretch like they've had a snack,
And each tree leans in for a good old hack.

A cat wearing slippers strolls down the lane,
Not a care in the world, no respect for the rain.
The moon pops out, a cheeky cheer,
Saying "Join the fun, there's nothing to fear!"

All the colors swirl, a mad maestro's hand,
Painting the town in a whimsical band.
With giggles and grins, the night becomes bright,
As dusk spins tales that ignite pure delight.

Radiance Above

Up in the sky, a circus parade,
With painted clouds, the sunset's charade.
A magician with flair, he pulls sunshine,
Turning plain evenings into a fine wine.

The birds are comedians, cracking their jokes,
While the sun plays along with all the folks.
It’s a spectacle bright, a festival feast,
With giggles and shouts, we all feel released.

A hippo in shades slides down a slide,
While butterflies flutter, all filled with pride.
The trees clap their hands, in cheer they embrace,
As day’s final act steals the whole space.

With laughter in torrents and joy to prolong,
This twilight show feels like a wild song.
So raise your glasses to the skies up high,
As the stars settle in for their glittering sky.

Ethereal Saffron

In twilight's glow, we dance like sprites,
The air is filled with hilarious bites.
As crickets play banjos, quite out of tune,
The moon laughs softly, a silvery boon.

A parade of ducks in tiny bow ties,
Waddling in rhythm, what a surprise!
The colors stretch out, a canvas anew,
With giggles echoing, we paint the view.

A cat on a skateboard rolls with delight,
Whipping around corners, oh what a sight!
With each passing moment, silliness reigns,
Under fluffy clouds, we shake off our chains.

As sun dips and chuckles float in the air,
We twirl and we spin, with naught a care.
The saffron hue wraps us snug in its fold,
As laughter unites us, bright and bold.

Potpourri of Dusk

The sun slips down with a wink,
Clouds swell slow, they start to stink.
A rabbit hops, says, "What a sight!"
Though I might trip, it's worth the fright.

A squirrel juggles acorns with glee,
While shadows dance like it’s a spree.
The trees wear hats made of last light,
As I laugh loud, it feels so right.

Fireflies twinkle, don’t you see?
They flash like bulbs, 'Look at me!'
The breeze hums jokes from days of yore,
I hold my belly, can’t take much more.

With dusk around, the fun won't cease,
Let’s roast a marshmallow, say, “Oh, please!”
The twilight bleeds with giggles, oh my!
In this funny dance, we dare to fly.

The Last Kiss of Sun

As the big bulb dips, it winks back,
Birds gather 'round for a breakfast snack.
A dog in shades lounges like a king,
While I trade stories with everything.

The sky blushes, then starts to giggle,
The breeze comes close, and starts to wiggle.
A cat dances on a fence, oh wow!
“Look at me, I’m a superstar now!”

With a last glow, the day’s on a spree,
A funny thought: what if it’s just me?
The clouds morph into shapes so silly,
I chuckle hard, it’s all too frilly.

The sun bows down with style and flair,
Magic in dusk is found everywhere.
So let’s toast to the day’s grand finale,
Where laughter reigns and joy's a rally.

Kissed by Fire

The day bids bye with a fiery grin,
Tickling clouds where fun begins.
A toaster pops, burns the bread, hooray!
I fumble, drop it, what a play.

The sky turns wild, like a kid set free,
Whispers secrets in a giggle spree.
A flamingo prances on a lawn,
With neon jokes that welcome dawn.

The laughter crackles, it's quite sublime,
Like popcorn popping in perfect time.
Who needs a stage? Just look above,
With fiery clouds that dance for love.

In this blaze, we toast to the night,
As fireflies twirl in sheer delight.
Let's make a wish on a spark so bright,
With giggles echoing, feels just right.

Melodies of Day's Retreat

As day fades out, the fun takes a cue,
The moon peeks in, with a hearty boo.
Crickets start their offbeat jam,
And I join in like a silly clam.

The horizon blushes, prancing around,
Clouds form harmonies, such a sound!
A raccoon steals my snack, oh dear!
I chase him down, fueled by good cheer.

With melodies light, the shadows play,
A serenade to end the day.
The stars dance like they're in a play,
And I laugh hard at this sweet ballet.

So let's hum tunes till the dark takes flight,
With every note, we'll dance in delight.
In this grand twilight, our hearts take wing,
As the world joins in, let the laughter ring.

A Symphony of Twilight

A trumpet blast from a far-off tune,
The sun wears shades like a goofball buffoon.
Clouds dance around in a glorious wedgie,
While birds bust out jokes, feeling quite edgy.

The trees start to giggle, their branches a-sway,
As squirrels crack up in a raucous ballet.
A pom-pom sunset steps into the light,
Giggling softly, it’s a sight quite bright.

The sky paints its laughter in splashes of cheer,
As shadows play tag, drawing near and near.
The breeze is a jester, with tricks up its sleeve,
In this comical world, we all can believe.

Burnished Dreams

A pancake sky with syrupy gleam,
Fluffy clouds toss flip-flops, or so it may seem.
The sun tosses confetti, what a funny sight,
As wishes ride piggyback, taking flight.

Marshmallow fluff floats amidst giggles galore,
While shadows attempt a dance on the floor.
Each ray of laughter crackles and pops,
As dreams hit the ground in delicious plops.

The horizon holds jokes that tickle the mind,
As bubblegum breezes leave worries behind.
We twirl in this whimsy, no frown to be found,
In a world painted bright, where fun knows no bounds.

The Last Light's Whisper

The sun spins tales in a whirl of delight,
As giggles from stars prepare for the night.
With a wink and a grin, it bids us adieu,
Leaving behind a canvas of the cheeriest hue.

The clouds turn into rabbits, oh what a jest!
They hop through the twilight; who could've guessed?
While shadows, like ninjas, sneak out of their lair,
Trying to blend in with the cool evening air.

The giggles of dusk wrap us snug like a hug,
As moonbeams bounce like a friendly slug.
This playful goodnight from the sky's silver crest,
Leaves us laughing and dreaming, oh what a jest!

Cinnamon-colored Serenade

A sprinkle of spice in the air, a flair,
As the horizon cracks up, unaware.
The sunset hums softly, a quirky old tune,
While fireflies twinkle in the gathering gloom.

Gingerbread clouds line dance in the breeze,
With cupcakes for stars, oh, what a tease!
The laughter of colors goes rolling away,
As jellybeans tumble to the end of the day.

The moon throws a party with snacks on the lawn,
While crickets play maracas, a chirping response.
In this sweet serenade, we'll sway and we'll spin,
Under cinnamon skies, let the fun begin!

A Brush of Sunfire

The sun splashed paint on the sleepy town,
While squirrels wear shades, trying not to frown.
The clouds get giggly, all fluffy and bright,
They bounce like jelly, a true silly sight.

A flamingo danced in the flaming hue,
Telling jokes to a cat, that was dressed in blue.
A dog wore a hat, claimed it was all style,
While pigeons in tuxedos watched all the while.

The trees started swaying, bent out of line,
They jived to the rhythm, thinking it's fine.
The sun laughed hard, with a twinkle and wink,
While kids built a pizza that smelled like a stink.

As the day got tired, still smiling so wide,
It tossed out a wink, then took a slide.
With a splat and a giggle, it dove down below,
Leaving behind a glow, oh what a show!

Sunset Allure

In a land where lemons jive with the lime,
The sky grabs a cup and spills out some rhyme.
With every sip, the clouds twist and twirl,
As geese play charades in a feathered whirl.

A cat in a parrot hat sings to the night,
While the moon sneaks a peek, feeling quite light.
A red fish in bowl starts to wiggle and roll,
Belting out secrets from the depths of his soul.

The stars now awake, they're ready to dance,
With trees playing tag, oh what a chance!
They trade goofy grins, in the twilight's embrace,
While shadows make faces, it’s a magical place.

As the fun fizzles out, with a splash and a pop,
The night takes a bow, then promises to stop.
But not before winking, with glitter so bright,
Leaving laughter behind, into the night.

Flames Beneath the Chrimson

A dragon in sunglasses took flight through the sky,
While birds donned sombreros, passing by.
They squawked lots of puns, had a laugh and a snack,
As they tumbled through colors, no hint of a lack.

With every burst of laughter, the sun's face glowed,
A parade of silliness, ready to explode.
The lake sparkled brightly, told tales of its depth,
Of turtles who moonwalked, with a bob and a step.

The flowers broke out in a conga line dance,
Begging the bees for a sweet little chance.
And as the breeze chuckled, with a shimmy and sway,
Even shadows joined in, turning night into day.

In the end, they all gathered for one final cheer,
As the sun did a curtsy and whispered, "I'll be near."
With giggles and glimmers, they waved goodbye,
To the colors of chaos, flitting on high.

Tides of Twilight

The ocean sighed softly, in shades nice and sweet,
As crabs held a barbecue, cooked up a treat.
Seagulls wore flip-flops, waddling around,
Making waves with their antics, oh what a sound!

On the sand, a starfish busted out a jig,
While clams played the banjo, feeling quite big.
The sun dipped low, with a giggle and grin,
As dolphins played tag, splashing in with a spin.

Sandcastles boogied, swaying left and right,
With flags made of seaweed, oh what a sight!
Each grain of sand whispered jokes to the tide,
As shadows crept closer, the day took a slide.

As night laid its blanket, the silliness swirled,
With fireflies twinkling, the laughter unfurled.
They danced on the waves, till the moon took its stand,
Leaving behind echoes of joy in the land.

The Day's Last Brush

As the sun dips down for a nap,
It paints the clouds with a funny slap.
Birds wear shades as they take flight,
Chasing laughs in the fading light.

Cats on roofs doing their dance,
Looking like they've got a chance.
While squirrels giggle, tails in the air,
With every joke they dare to share.

The world turns bright with a cheeky grin,
Nature's folly, a merry spin.
Colors clash like friends in a fight,
Throwing a party, oh what a sight!

As night rolls in with a sleepy cheer,
Fireflies chuckle, "We made it here!"
So grab your snacks, let's toast the day,
To the humor found in the sunset's play.

Crimson Whispers

The sun winks low, whispers sweet cheer,
Clouds gossip like they've had a beer.
A tangerine cat in the garden will prance,
While butterflies boast about their dance.

Silly shadows stretch long and lean,
Tickling the grass, oh what a scene!
Laughter erupts from the trees nearby,
As squirrels pretend they are flying high.

With splashes of scarlet, it's pure delight,
Even the breeze knows how to be bright.
The sun's going down but the fun's just begun,
In this vibrant laugh, we're all number one!

So grab your friends, and let's take a ride,
Under a canvas where giggles abide.
The sky may fade but the humor won't flee,
As long as we're together, it's blissfully free.

Hues of the Fading Light

With a wink from the sun, the colors collide,
A sunset that dances, oh what a ride!
The neighbors yell jokes from their porches wide,
While kids armed with chalk take the sidewalk's side.

Peeking through clouds in a whimsical show,
The flamingo costumes make quite the glow!
Fireflies burst forth in a twinkly parade,
While all of the puppies are eager to play.

The horizon's a canvas where laughter takes flight,
As crickets hold concerts in the fading light.
Every hue steeped in giggles, and shed of their shame,
What a sight to behold, this colorful game!

So come one, come all, let your spirits ignite,
In hues that defy all the rules of the night.
With laughter as our guide in this whimsical flight,
Together we'll dance till the moon says goodnight.

Phoenix on the Horizon

From the horizon, a fiery figment,
Pokes out its head, chuckling with intent.
It seems to shout, “What a glorious mess!”
While clouds just blush in a funny dress.

Balloons float high in a silly parade,
All dressed up, ready to serenade.
The sun plays tricks with a warm, golden wink,
As ducks wear ties, they swim and they sink.

Bright oranges tease with their giggly hues,
Making everyone take a moment to snooze.
While trees sway along to their favorite tune,
As shadows prance under a plump pink moon.

The day bows out with a whimsical kick,
Leaving behind a sparkle, a flick.
With laughter still ringing in the twilight’s embrace,
The phoenix takes flight, leaving joy in its trace.

The Ember Poem

A cat in shades, it strikes a pose,
He flicks his tail and gently dozes.
With fireflies buzzing, he starts to dance,
In the funny light, he takes a chance.

A bird in specs, with a quirky strut,
Sips from a pond, thinks it's a hut.
Winks at the sky, then trips on a root,
Laughs aloud, in a glorious suit.

A pair of frogs, on lily pads,
Join the party, looking quite rad.
They croak a tune, so off-key and wild,
But hop along, like a silly child.

As night rolls in, the giggles flee,
But every twinkle whispers, "Let it be!"
In the closing act, all creatures defy,
With a bow to the dusk, and a wink to the sky.

Twilight Interlude

The sun bows out, it's time to gleam,
A duck in a tux dreams of ice cream.
He quacks a tune, and the cows join in,
As giggles bloom, where chaos begins.

A squirrel on stilts, oh what a sight,
He tumbles and rolls, in pure delight.
With nuts in hand, he prances around,
In this weightless wonder, where fun is found.

Kids ride bikes with balloons all around,
That pop like dreams, as laughter's found.
They race the stars, and twirl with glee,
As night takes over, wild and free.

A hop, a skip, then a joyous twirl,
The twilight knows the magic swirl.
With a wink from the stars, they call it a day,
And take their laughter, in dreams, to play.

The Slow Flame of Dusk

Two fireflies dance in a game of tag,
One bumps a bug, they both just wag.
A light so silly, they chuckle away,
As the world grows dim, they seize the play.

A raccoon dons glasses, reading a book,
On chapters of snack, give it a look!
He guffaws aloud, at every plot twist,
In the laughter's hold, nothing's missed.

With shadows stretching, the crickets tune in,
Their chirpy chatter begins to spin.
A frog joins in wearing a tiny crown,
Sings of his reign all over town!

As dusk takes hold, the giggles rise,
With a wink and a nod, the critters surprise.
In the slow flame glow, they dance and sway,
In this nightly comedy, they find their way.

Day’s Affair with Dusk

The sun gives a wink, says its goodbye,
A chicken in shades puffs out with pride.
It struts down the lane, clucking a tune,
As shadows grow long beneath the moon.

A cow with a scarf twirls in delight,
Doing the cha-cha, what a sight!
With a hop and a flap, she dances near,
Spreading the giggles, bringing good cheer.

There’s mischief and laughter in the air,
As crickets hold hands without a care.
They trip and tumble as fireflies glow,
While the sky fades soft, putting on a show.

And as the curtain drops on day,
They steal the spotlight, come out to play.
In the affair of dusk, they're here to stay,
With funny tales that brighten the gray.

A Canvas Aflame

The painter tripped, his brush took flight,
Splashed the world in hues of light.
A cat danced past, knocked over paint,
Now the dog wears a dip-dyed faint.

With wobbly strokes, he made a deer,
But it looks more like a cave-dwelling sphere.
The canvas giggles, colors bright,
As squirrels hold a paintbrush tight.

A parrot squawks a clever phrase,
As the artist stumbles in a daze.
He laughs, as he spills a bit of blue,
Turns the mess into a caribou.

The finished piece, a wacky scene,
Of dancing frogs in a tangerine sheen.
Even the trees are laughing loud,
At the silly world he has avowed.

Softness of the Setting Sun

The sun slipped down with a wink and grin,
It’s playing hide and seek again.
Clouds puffed up like cotton candy,
While evening bugs start a band-y.

A squirrel cracks jokes on a branch,
While dusk delivers an evening dance.
Cackling frogs in a lily pad choir,
Hoping to catch the last sun's fire.

The picnic ants march in a line,
We're never late, they'll say, it’s fine!
But ketchup spills as they slide and race,
Now they’re stuck in a sticky place!

The shadows stretch, the colors blend,
And laughter rises, as sunsets tend.
In this cozy world of playful light,
It's hard to tell if it's day or night.

Fields of Flame

In fields where the poppies dance and sway,
Butterflies giggle at hide-and-seek play.
A scarecrow spins, then trips on a shoe,
With pants so bright, they must be brand new!

The rabbits hop in a moda vivace,
Wearing shades, looking suave, quite brassy.
But watch out for birds making plans,
They've brought along some popcorn cans!

A bee buzzes by, so chubby and grand,
Trying to pull off a cool dessert stand.
He spills the honey, makes quite a mess,
Now the flowers are in a sticky dress!

So come for the fun in the golden light,
Where critters tease as they frolic in flight.
Laughter echoes in fields once so tame,
Now joyfully wild, all part of the game.

The Ember Trail

A trail of sparks led us astray,
Chasing fireflies in a whimsical play.
We stumbled upon a marshmallow buffet,
Careful not to roast our fingers, oh yay!

Ghost stories told by glowing red light,
As frogs in tuxedos leap with delight.
A raccoon with a top hat joins the fun,
Stealing snacks from everyone one by one!

The moon rises high, joins our crew,
Wearing a smile like it always knew.
While shadows twirl to the campfire's sway,
Even the crickets have come out to play!

With laughter that crackles like wood in the heat,
The ember trail brings memories sweet.
Though the night grows dark, we shine like a star,
In this silly world, we’ve come very far.

www.ingramcontent.com/pod-product-compliance
Lightning Source LLC
Chambersburg PA
CBHW070314120526
44590CB00017B/2674
9781805867401